EXPLORING DINOSAURS

OVIRAPTOR

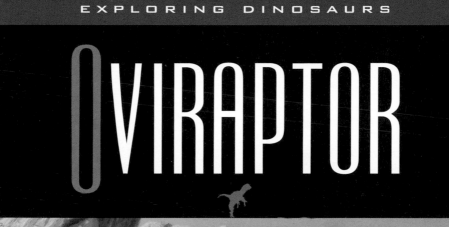

By Susan H. Gray

THE CHILD'S WORLD®
CHANHASSEN, MINNESOTA

Content Adviser:
Peter Makovicky,
Ph.D., Curator,
Field Museum,
Chicago, Illinois

Published in the United States of America by The Child's World®
PO Box 326, Chanhassen, MN 55317-0326
800-599-READ
www.childsworld.com

Photo Credits: American Museum of Natural History: 4, 9, 12, 18, 20; Corbis: 5 (Annie Griffiths Belt), 9 (Hulton-Deutsch Collection), 11 (Bettmann), 14 (Layne Kennedy), 15 (Jim Zuckerman), 27 (Reuters NewMedia Inc.); Custom Medical Stock Photo: 8; Douglas Henderson: 23; Michael Skrepnick: 6, 25; Mike Fredericks: 7, 16; Photo Researchers/Science Photo Library: 21 (Worldsat International/J. Knighton), 22 (Chris Butler); Todd Marshall: 17.

The Child's World®: Mary Berendes, Publishing Director

Editorial Directions, Inc.: E. Russell Primm, Editorial Director; Ruth M. Martin, Line Editor; Katie Marsico, Assistant Editor; Matthew Messbarger, Editorial Assistant; Susan Hindman, Copy Editor; Susan Ashley, Proofreader; Tim Griffin, Indexer; Kerry Reid, Fact Checker; Cian Loughlin O'Day, Photo Reseacher; Linda S. Koutris, Photo Selector

Original cover art by Todd Marshall

The Design Lab: Kathleen Petelinsek, Design and Art Direction; Kari Thornborough, Page Production

Library of Congress Cataloging-in-Publication Data
Gray, Susan Heinrichs.
  Oviraptor / by Susan H. Gray.
    p. cm. — (Exploring dinosaurs)
Includes index.
Summary: Describes what is known about the physical characteristics, behavior, habitat, and life cycle of this small, bird-like dinosaur.
  ISBN 1-59296-189-4 (lib. bdg. : alk. paper)
  1. Oviraptor—Juvenile literature. [1. Oviraptor. 2. Dinosaurs.] I. Title. II. Series.
QE862.S3G6955 2004
567.912—dc22   2003018628

TABLE OF CONTENTS

CHAPTER ONE

FAITHFUL TO THE END

Little *Oviraptor* (OH-vih-RAP-tur) squinted her eyes. The wind was growing stronger. Dust and sand were flying everywhere.

Sand grains blew across her face. She shut her eyes tight and lowered her head. Her eyes stung and began to water.

The wind roared and the sandstorm grew fierce. But the little dinosaur did not budge. Instead, she settled more securely into her

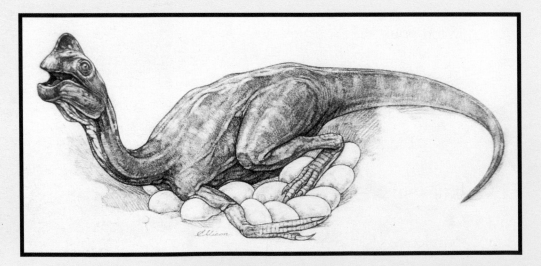

By sitting on her nest, the mother Oviraptor *protected her eggs. During the day, she would have provided shade from the scorching desert sun. As it got colder during the night, her body would have helped the eggs to stay warm.*

nest. Just beneath her were 15 eggs. Inside each one, a baby *Oviraptor* was growing.

The howl of the wind became even louder. The air was so filled with sand that the sky grew dark. The mother dinosaur tried to shield the eggs with her body. Sand swept up against the side of the nest. It covered *Oviraptor*'s back and arms. The sand slowly rose higher. Soon only her neck and head were showing above the sand.

Wind pounded the little dinosaur. But *Oviraptor* did not leave her eggs. The sand crept slowly up her neck, then buried her completely. Helpless, *Oviraptor* took her last breath and died.

Sandstorms where the Oviraptor *lived were both sudden and severe. An* Oviraptor *could be buried trying to protect her nest.*

CHAPTER TWO

WHAT IS AN OVIRAPTOR?

An *Oviraptor* is a dinosaur that lived from about 88 million to 70 million years ago. Its name is taken from Latin words that mean "egg robber." It was given this name because scientists first believed that *Oviraptor* ate the eggs of other dinosaurs.

From its snout to the tip of its tail, an adult was about 6 to 8 feet (1.8 to 2.4 meters) long. The **reptile** weighed around 55 to 75 pounds (25 to 34 kilograms) and stood about 3 feet (0.9 m) tall. *Oviraptor*

This is a picture of what a young Oviraptor *might have looked like. He looks cute, but watch out—his claws and sharp beak are very dangerous!*

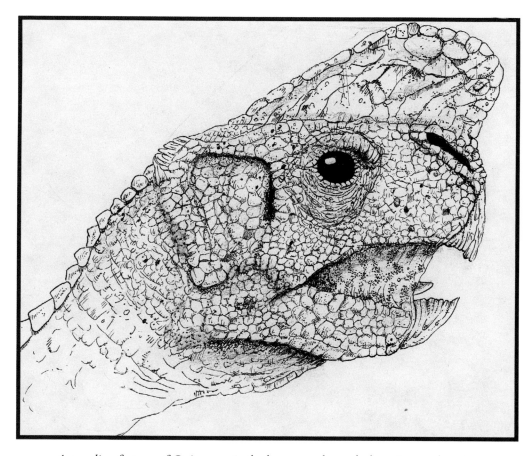

A peculiar feature of Oviraptor *is the bony crest located above its nasal cavity. Scientists have many theories about what it was used for. Some scientists believe* Oviraptor *may have used its crest to amplify sound. Today, Southeast Asian birds known as hornbills use a similar crest (called a casque) to magnify their own calls.*

could run quickly on its two back legs, perhaps up to 40 miles

(64 kilometers) per hour in short bursts.

At the end of *Oviraptor*'s arms were strong hands that could

grab and hold things. The hands had three very long fingers, each with a sharp, curved claw. The reptile's tail was thick and barely

reached the ground. Usually the dinosaur held its tail straight out

in back as it walked or ran.

Oviraptor's skeleton was very lightweight because its bones

were filled with holes. Even its skull was not solid. Some bones

were so full of holes, they looked spongy. Its lightweight skeleton

and powerful legs made the dinosaur a fast runner.

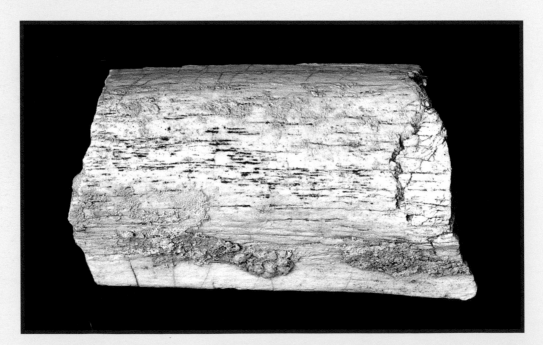

Lightweight bones could have been a great advantage for Oviraptor,
giving it the speed it needed to escape from bigger dinosaurs.

CHAPTER THREE

WHO FOUND THE FIRST *OVIRAPTOR?*

George Olsen was with a team of scientists when he discovered *Oviraptor.* They were working in Mongolia's Gobi (GO-bee) Desert. It was the 1920s, and the team was led by Roy Chapman Andrews. Andrews was an explorer and paleontologist (PAY-lee-un-TAWL-uh-jist). Paleontologists study **ancient** plants and animals. His team was in the desert looking for fossils and other interesting things that could help them learn about Earth long ago.

Roy Chapman Andrews had a reputation for getting into dangerous situations and is said to have inspired the movie character Indiana Jones. While he was an explorer, Andrews spent two weeks stranded on a deserted island, was shipwrecked in shark-infested waters, and accidentally camped in a den of 47 poisonous snakes!

Unfortunately, their life in the desert was miserable. The wind was so strong that it tore the men's shirts off. Blowing sand ripped their flesh until it bled. The afternoon heat made them sick. Nighttime temperatures were close to freezing. Poisonous snakes slithered into the men's tents as they slept.

In 1922, Andrews and his team ventured out into previously unexplored parts of the Gobi Desert, using some of the region's first automobiles. Along the way, they braved vicious sandstorms and heavily armed bandits.

Still, the scientists worked on. They searched valleys and hills.

They trekked over sand dunes. They kept on despite the hardships.

Finally, their work paid off. One man found the skeleton of a

giant rhinoceros. Others

found dinosaur bones. Then

one day, George Olsen

returned to camp saying he

had found some **fossilized**

eggs. Andrews did not believe

it at first. But then he went

with Olsen to see for himself.

At a place called the Flaming

Cliffs, they found not only

eggs, but also a small

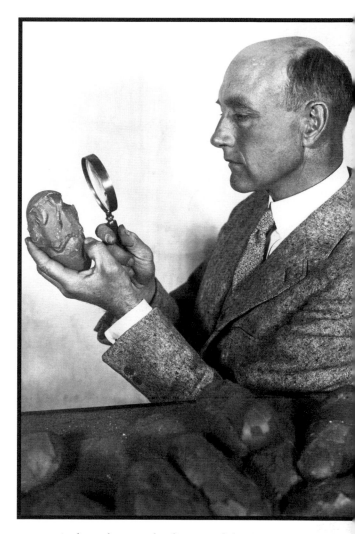

Andrews became the director of the American Museum of Natural History in 1941. He wrote many books about his explorations.

dinosaur skeleton. The scientists believed that the little dinosaur

had been raiding another dinosaur's nest when it died. Thinking

it was an egg thief, they gave it the name *Oviraptor*.

Seventy years later, paleontologists were again exploring the

Gobi Desert. They found another *Oviraptor* skeleton. This one

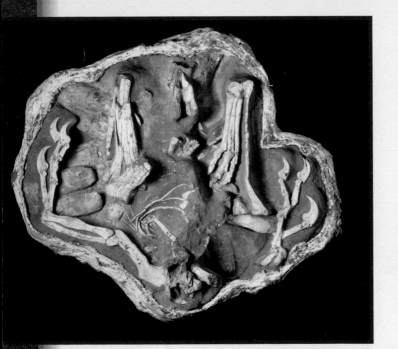

had its arms spread over a

nest of eggs. The scientists

realized these were really

Oviraptor eggs. Suddenly,

everyone saw the dinosaur

in a new way. It was not a

nest raider at all. It had

eggs of its own and died

protecting them.

In 1993, paleontologists discovered a fossil in Mongolia that gave new clues to the true nature of Oviraptor. *The fossil contained an* Oviraptor *skeleton atop its eggs. Mark Norell, one of the paleontologists who was there, helped show that* Oviraptor *was not eating the eggs. With this new evidence, paleontologists now believe that* Oviraptor *was a protective parent.*

STUCK WITH A BAD NAME

Imagine that you have discovered a new kind of dinosaur. You are the first person in the world to see it. You can't believe your good luck, and you're dying to tell everyone.

This is probably how the men on Roy Chapman Andrews's team felt when they first saw *Oviraptor.* It's how most paleontologists feel when they discover a new animal. They can't wait to tell the world.

But telling the world is not easy. Scientists must follow strict rules when they do this. First, they check all the official books and lists to make sure the animal was not discovered already. Then they describe everything about the new creature. If it's a dinosaur, they measure the bones and count the fingers and toes. They look closely at the teeth. They try to figure out what the animal ate. They write down where it was found, and they take lots of pictures. They also pick out a name for the dinosaur—one that tells something about it.

Sometimes, during all of this, animals get stuck with the wrong names. At first, everyone believed *Oviraptor* was a thief. But skeletons discovered more than 70 years later showed something different. The little dinosaur was really an egg protector. But it was too late. *Oviraptor* was already stuck with its bad name.

CHAPTER FOUR

WHAT DID
Oviraptor EAT?

O*viraptor* was probably an omnivore (AHM-nih-vore). This means that it ate both plants and animals. Its diet may have included fruits, eggs, shellfish, meat, and leaves.

Most dinosaurs were not omnivores. Many were carnivores (KAR-nih-vores), meaning they ate only meat. Carnivores had sharp claws for killing animals and sharp teeth for tearing them apart. Most other dinosaurs were herbi-vores (UR-buh-vores), meaning

T-rex, *like* Oviraptor, *was in the group of dinosaurs known as the theropods. Theropods had big and powerful birdlike legs and small arms.*

they ate only plants. They had no need of sharp claws. They had broad, bumpy teeth for grinding up leaves and twigs.

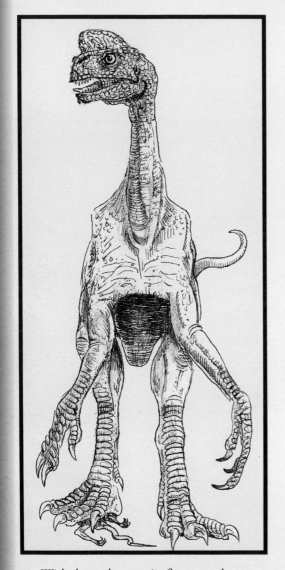

With sharp claws on its fingers and toes, a tough beak, strong jaws, and quick, agile legs, Oviraptor *was built for tracking down and eating all sorts of things.*

Why do paleontologists think *Oviraptor* was an omnivore? The dinosaur's skeleton holds the clues. Scientists think that *Oviraptor*'s long legs probably helped it chase down **prey.** Its long, clawed fingers could have helped it tear meat apart. Its strong jaws could have cracked clam shells. Its hard beak would have been perfect for tearing plants apart. And, because the animal was so small and close to the ground, it could have snapped up insects and eggs. In other words, *Oviraptor* was built for eating all kinds of things.

Very large dinosaurs spent most of their time eating. Some had to eat hundreds of pounds of food every day. But not *Oviraptor*. Because it was small, it got by on much less. It probably ate just a few quick meals and snacks a day.

Big carnivores such as Neovenator *(NEE-oh-ven-AY-tor), had to eat often and needed to consume large amounts of food to stay full.*

CHAPTER FIVE

WHERE DID
Oviraptor LIVE?

So far, we know of only one country where *Oviraptor* lived. That country is Mongolia. Someday, *Oviraptor* might be found elsewhere. But almost a century has passed since the first discovery, and no one has found the dinosaur anywhere else.

The fossils found in southern Mongolia are made up mostly of animals, including birds and dinosaurs, that lived some 80 million years ago during the late Cretaceous period. This was about 15 million years before the dinosaurs disappeared. Fossilized dinosaurs such as this Oviraptor *have made Mongolia one of the richest places on Earth for fossil hunting.*

Many other kinds of dinosaurs have been found in Mongolia. In fact, the country is a favorite place for fossil hunters. What makes it so special?

In Mongolia, the **environment** is just right for fossils to survive. When dinosaurs died, different things could happen to their bodies. Some were eaten by other dinosaurs. Some were washed away by floods. Some just rotted to pieces. These dinosaurs would have left nothing behind.

However, other dinosaurs died and were quickly buried in sand, mud, or volcanic ash. Nothing could eat these dinosaurs. Bacteria did not cause them to rot. And these buried dinosaurs could not blow away or wash away.

The Gobi Desert in Mongolia is the perfect place to preserve dinosaur bones. Mongolian dinosaurs were probably caught in flash floods, sandstorms, and collapsing sand dunes. They were

buried in mud or hot sand. Their skeletons remained untouched

for centuries. Now, scientists are finding them.

Even though it is one of the best places in the world to find well-preserved dinosaur fossils, paleontologist expeditions to Mongolia require an enormous amount of time, patience, and money. Paleontologists must navigate through uncharted territory, a land with no roads and no maps, as they search for fossils that remain hidden.

A NEW WAY TO HUNT FOSSILS

Looking for fossils has always meant spending long hours outdoors. In places like the Gobi Desert, fossil hunting is especially tough. The desert is huge and the weather is bad. There are no gas stations or grocery stores. Tents and camping equipment get blown away and buried. Paleontologists in the Gobi draw maps to remember where they've seen fossils. But then sandstorms come and change everything. Roads and pathways get covered up. Landmarks blow away.

Now, some paleontologists are trying a new way to find fossils. Before they ever set foot in the desert, they look at photographs taken by **satellite.** A satellite called Landsat circles high above Earth, shooting pictures of the planet. It transmits them back to scientists on the ground.

Paleontologists study Landsat pictures of the Gobi Desert. From the photos, they find the areas most likely to have fossils. Then they know right where to go when they arrive at the desert. This saves days of driving, walking, and searching.

CHAPTER SIX

WHEN DID
Oviraptor LIVE?

Oviraptor lived during a time called the Cretaceous (kreh-TAY-shuss) period. The entire period lasted from about 144 million to 65 million years ago. *Oviraptor* lived during the last part of the period.

Scientists think of the Cretaceous period as the heyday of the dinosaurs. This means that dinosaurs thrived during this time. Dinosaurs such as Tyrannosaurus rex and Triceratops appeared, as did many others.

What was the Cretaceous period anyway? Why don't we just say that *Oviraptor* lived millions of years ago? Why do we need to call it the Cretaceous period?

Phrases such as "Cretaceous period" help scientists talk about time. Think about the words you use to talk about time. You talk

Very early dinosaurs include Pisanosaurus *that lived in Argentina more than 200 million years ago.*

about your mornings, afternoons, weekends, and summers. You use such words because these times are important to you. You do different things at each of these different times.

Scientists are the same way. They know that life has been on Earth for millions of years. They know that living things have changed a lot over the years. They know that the climate, land, and oceans have changed, too.

Scientists have given names to the different stages of Earth's history. This helps them imagine how the world looked at different times. Scientists believe that dinosaurs first appeared around 225 million years ago during the Triassic period. Early dinosaurs were small animals, not the giants we usually picture. Earth was fairly warm at that time. Ferns and mosses covered the ground.

Next, during the Jurassic period, many large dinosaurs appeared. Reptiles flew through the skies and swam in the oceans. Small, ratlike mammals ran around on the ground.

During the Cretaceous period, oak and maple trees sprang up. Birds soared through the air. *Oviraptor* trotted around in Mongolia. By the end of the period, *Oviraptor* and all the other dinosaurs had disappeared.

During the late Cretaceous period, Pteranodons *(meaning "winged and toothless") flew through the air.* Pteranodons *were flying reptiles that hunted fish, mollusks, and crabs.*

The dinosaurs lived through three long periods of Earth's history.

The words *Triassic, Jurassic,* and *Cretaceous* help scientists—and us—

imagine the world at those different times.

CHAPTER SEVEN

WHY DID THE DINOSAURS DISAPPEAR?

No one is quite sure why the dinosaurs became **extinct**.

But by the end of the Cretaceous period, they were all

gone. Dinosaurs were not the only animals to disappear. Flying

reptiles also died out. The swimming reptiles of the sea vanished

as well. Different plant forms died, too.

Scientists have several ideas about why this great extinction

took place. Some believe that lots of volcanoes erupted at the time.

Perhaps volcanic ash and fumes polluted the air too much for plants

and animals to live. Other scientists say that mammals were eating

all the dinosaur eggs. Perhaps this caused the dinosaurs to die out.

Some scientists think that a giant **asteroid** crashed into Earth.

As it did, dust and ash rose into the air for miles around. Sunlight could barely shine through it. Without enough sunlight, plants died. Because of this, plant-eating animals also died. Then the animals that ate *them* died. By the time the dust settled, the dino-saurs were history.

Many scientists believe that an asteroid slammed into the earth about 65 million years ago. This would have devastated the environment and led to the mass extinction of plant and animal life.

We may never know exactly what happened. In fact, there are many things we don't know about the dinosaurs. What was *Oviraptor*'s favorite food? Why did it have that crest? And did it *ever* steal other dinosaurs' eggs? Plenty of questions remain. Maybe you'll grow up to be the scientist who can answer them.

Glossary

ancient (AYN-shunt) Something that is ancient is very old; from millions of years ago. Paleontologists study ancient forms of plant and animal life.

asteroid (ASS-tuh-royd) An asteroid is a rocky body that is smaller than a planet and orbits the Sun. A giant asteroid may have crashed into Earth millions of years ago and caused the dinosaurs to die out.

environment (en-VYE-ruhn-muhnt) An environment is made up of the things that surround a living creature, such as the air and soil. In Mongolia, the environment is just right for fossils to survive.

extinct (ek-STINGKT) Something that is extinct no longer exists. The dinosaurs became extinct.

fossilized (FOSS-uhl-eyezed) Something that is fossilized became a fossil. Scientists might find fossilized teeth and claws as a part of a dinosaur's remains.

prey (PRAY) Prey are animals that are hunted and eaten by other animals. Scientists think that *Oviraptor's* long legs probably helped it chase down prey.

reptile (REP-tile) A reptile is an air-breathing animal with a backbone and is usually covered with scales or plates. *Oviraptor* was an example of a reptile.

satellite (SAT-uh-leyet) A satellite is something that orbits, or circles, a planet. Landsat is a satellite that takes pictures of Earth's surface.

Did You Know?

▸ Like *Oviraptor,* some birds today have big crests on their heads. The birds use these to make loud noises.

▸ The average third-grader is taller than an adult *Oviraptor.*

▸ Roy Chapman Andrews and his team of scientists ran into bandits and warring tribes in the Gobi Desert.

The Geologic Time Scale

TRIASSIC PERIOD

Date: 248 million to 208 million years ago

Fossils: *Coelophysis, Cynodont, Desmatosuchus, Eoraptor, Gerrothorax, Peteinosaurus, Placerias, Plateosaurus, Postosuchus, Procompsognathus, Riojasaurus, Saltopus, Teratosaurus, Thecodontosaurus*

Distinguishing Features: For the most part, the climate in the Triassic period was hot and dry. The first true mammals appeared during this period, as well as turtles, frogs, salamanders, and lizards. Corals could also be found in oceans at this time, although large reefs such as the ones we have today did not yet exist. Evergreen trees made up much of the plant life.

JURASSIC PERIOD

Date: 208 million to 144 million years ago

Fossils: *Allosaurus, Anchisaurus, Apatosaurus, Barosaurus, Brachiosaurus, Ceratosaurus, Compsognathus, Cryptoclidus, Dilophosaurus, Diplodocus, Eustreptospondylus, Hybodus, Janenschia, Kentrosaurus, Liopleurodon, Megalosaurus, Opthalmosaurus, Rhamphorhynchus, Saurolophus, Segisaurus, Seismosaurus, Stegosaurus, Supersaurus, Syntarsus, Ultrasaurus, Vulcanodon, Xiaosaurus*

Distinguishing Features: The climate of the Jurassic period was warm and moist. The first birds appeared during this period. Plant life was also greener and more widespread. Sharks began swimming in Earth's oceans. Although dinosaurs didn't even exist at the beginning of the Triassic period, they ruled Earth by Jurassic times. There was a minor mass extinction toward the end of the Jurassic period.

CRETACEOUS PERIOD

Date: 144 million to 65 million years ago

Fossils: *Acrocanthosaurus, Alamosaurus, Albertosaurus, Anatotitan, Ankylosaurus, Argentinosaurus, Bagaceratops, Baryonyx, Carcharodontosaurus, Carnotaurus, Centrosaurus, Chasmosaurus, Corythosaurus, Didelphodon, Edmontonia, Edmontosaurus, Gallimimus, Gigantosaurus, Hadrosaurus, Hypsilophodon, Iguanodon, Kronosaurus, Lambeosaurus, Leaellynasaura, Maiasaura, Megaraptor, Muttaburrasaurus, Nodosaurus, Ornithocheirus, Oviraptor, Pachycephalosaurus, Panoplosaurus, Parasaurolophus, Pentaceratops, Polacanthus, Protoceratops, Psittacosaurus, Quaesitosaurus, Saltasaurus, Sarcosuchus, Saurolophus, Sauropelta, Saurornithoides, Segnosaurus, Spinosaurus, Stegoceras, Stygimoloch, Styracosaurus, Tapejara, Tarbosaurus, Therizinosaurus, Thescelosaurus, Torosaurus, Trachodon, Triceratops, Troodon, Tyrannosaurus rex, Utahraptor, Velociraptor*

Distinguishing Features: The climate of the Cretaceous period was fairly mild. Flowering plants first appeared in this period, and many modern plants developed. With flowering plants came a greater diversity of insect life. Birds further developed into two types: flying and flightless. A wider variety of mammals also existed. At the end of this period came a great mass extinction that wiped out the dinosaurs, along with several other groups of animals.

How to Learn More

At the Library

Norell, Mark A., Lowell Dingus, and Mick Ellison (illustrator).
A Nest of Dinosaurs: The Story of Oviraptor. New York: Doubleday, 1999.

White, David, and Pam Mara (illustrator).
Oviraptor. Vero Beach, Fla.: The Rourke Book Company, Inc., 1989.

On the Web

Visit our home page for lots of links about *Oviraptor:*
http://www.childsworld.com/links.html
Note to Parents, Teachers, and Librarians: We routinely verify our
Web links to make sure they're safe, active sites—so encourage
your readers to check them out!

Places to Visit or Contact

AMERICAN MUSEUM OF NATURAL HISTORY
To see several exhibits related to Oviraptor
Central Park West at 79th Street
New York, NY 10024-5192
212/769-5100

CARNEGIE MUSEUM OF NATURAL HISTORY
*To view a variety of dinosaur skeletons, as well as fossils related
to other reptiles, amphibians, and fish that are now extinct*
4400 Forbes Avenue
Pittsburgh, PA 15213
412/622-3131

DINOSAUR NATIONAL MONUMENT
To view a huge deposit of dinosaur bones in a natural setting
Dinosaur, CO 81610-9724
or
Dinosaur National Monument (Quarry)
11625 East 1500 South
Jensen, UT 84035
435/781-7700

MUSEUM OF THE ROCKIES
To see real dinosaur fossils, as well as robotic replicas
Montana State University
600 West Kagy Boulevard
Bozeman, MT 59717-2730
406/994-2251 or 406/994-DINO (3466)

NATIONAL MUSEUM OF NATURAL HISTORY
(SMITHSONIAN INSTITUTION)
To see several dinosaur exhibits and special behind-the-scenes tours
10th Street and Constitution Avenue, N.W.
Washington, D.C. 20560-0166
202/357-2700

Index

About the Author

Susan H. Gray has bachelor's and master's degrees in zoology, and has taught college-level courses in biology. She first fell in love with fossil hunting while studying paleontology in college. In her 25 years as an author, she has written many articles for scientists and researchers, and many science books for children. Susan enjoys gardening, traveling, and playing the piano. She and her husband, Michael, live in Cabot, Arkansas.